Careers in Drone Technology

Joshua Gregory

Published in the United States of America by
Cherry Lake Publishing, Ann Arbor, Michigan
www.cherrylakepublishing.com

Reading Adviser: Marla Conn, MS, Ed., Literacy specialist, Read-Ability, Inc.

Photo Credits: Cover, LaineN; page 4 (left), eHrach; Page 4 (right), Riksa Prayogi; page 6, sezer66; page 8, Suwin; page 10, Beros919; page 12, BNMK0819; page 14, FakeStocker; page 16, Myvisuals; page 18, RomanR; page 20, sklyareek; page 22, REDPIXEL.PL; page 24, Solis Images; page 26, Aleksandr Markin; page 28, Zoom Team. Source: Shutterstock.

Library of Congress Cataloging-in-Publication Data

CIP data has been filed and is available at catalog.loc.gov.

Printed in the United States of America.

Table of Contents

Hello, Emerging Tech Careers!

In the past ...

Groundbreaking inventions made life easier in many ways.

In the present ...

New technologies are changing the world in mind-boggling ways.

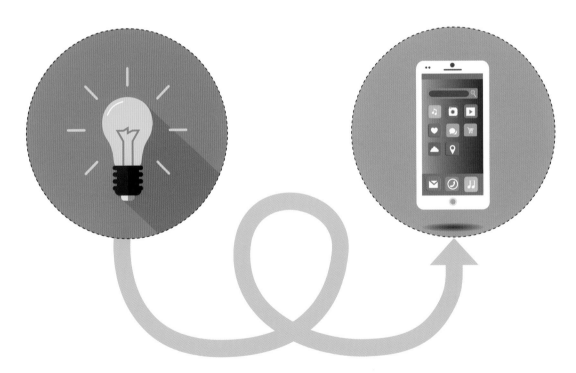

The future is yours to imagine!

WHAT COMES NEXT?

Who would have thought?

Alexander Graham Bell invented the first telephone in 1876. In 1879, Thomas Edison invented the first electric lightbulb. The Wright brothers successfully flew the first airplane in 1903. And don't forget Henry Ford! He invented a way to make cars quicker and cheaper.

These brilliant inventors did things that people once thought were impossible. To go from candles to electricity? From horse-drawn carriages to automobiles and airplanes? Wow!

The sky's the limit!

Now technology is being used to do even more amazing things! Take **drones**, for instance. A drone is an unmanned aerial vehicle (UAV) that is navigated by remote control or special software. Many people have toy drones that they fly for fun. More powerful drones are used by the military, for traffic and weather monitoring, search and rescue operations, firefighting, and package delivery.

This book explores the people and professions behind drones. Some of these careers, like UAV pilot, are so cutting-edge that they didn't exist just a decade or so ago. Others, like mechanical engineer, offer exciting new twists using drones.

Read on to explore exciting possibilities for your future!

Aerospace Engineer

You hear a buzzing sound in the air above you and look up. Some kind of vehicle is zipping through the sky. It's too small to be a helicopter or an airplane. In fact, it's too small to even carry a passenger. Could it be a drone?

You've probably heard a lot about drones. You may have even flown one yourself. These flying vehicles come in all kinds of shapes and sizes. Often, they are used for important jobs such as military missions or delivering packages to remote areas. Other times, they are just for fun. People have been building drones for decades. However, thanks to the efforts of talented engineers, drone technology has improved a great deal in recent years.

Engineers who specialize in aircraft are called aerospace engineers. Aerospace engineers use their knowledge of physics to think about the ways different objects can move through air. They might test out different wing shapes to see which ones make an aircraft fly fastest. They might experiment with the size and placement of rotors to improve an aircraft's ability to lift heavy things. They might also work with different materials to create vehicles that weigh less or don't require as much energy to fly.

Imagine It!

→ Build a paper airplane and throw it a few times. What do you notice about its flight? What can you do to improve it?

→ Make another airplane, but do it differently. For example, use heavier paper or give your airplane a different shape. Find all kinds of ideas at www.Foldnfly.com.

→ Make a chart to keep track of what features work best.

Dig Deeper!

✓ Check out this National Aeronautics and Space Administration (NASA) web page to learn more about the science behind flight: http://bit.ly/AeroNASA.

✓ You can also read about the way helicopter-style rotors work: http://bit.ly/NASACopter.

Aerospace engineers design drones for special purposes like agriculture.

Most drones look and function a lot like other aircraft. Because of this similarity, many of the same skills that aerospace engineers use to design airplanes or helicopters can be applied to drone technology. Some drones have wings and engines that allow them to take off like airplanes. Other have spinning rotors that work like the blades on a helicopter. So what sets drones apart from these other types of aircraft? A drone's most amazing feature is that it doesn't need a pilot onboard to control it. Instead, the pilot stays behind on the ground and operates the drone from a distance. For this reason, drones are also known as unmanned aerial vehicles, or UAVs.

Thanks to the work of aerospace engineers, today's drones are smaller, lighter, and easier to use than ever before. Such improvements have led them to become a common sight around the world. It will be amazing to see what these amazing engineers come up with next!

Future Aerospace Engineer

If you want to become an aerospace engineer, you'll need a college degree. In the meantime, you should do your best to learn about the science of flight. You'll need a strong understanding of physics as well as general engineering concepts. One great way to get a handle on the basics is to build your own drone from a kit.

Artificial Intelligence Researcher

You had a great time playing with your drone yesterday. But this morning, you realized that you can't remember where you left it when you were done flying. It's no problem, though. You open the drone **app** on your phone and press a single button. Seconds later, you see the drone flying toward you.

Believe it or not, many drones are already able to find their way home if their pilots lose track of them. Some can do other smart things without humans telling them to. They might be able to automatically avoid obstacles in their path. They might even be able to find a location and fly to it without a human pilot steering.

These drones' amazing abilities are controlled by something called **artificial intelligence**, or AI. This doesn't mean they are as smart as people or that they can think for themselves all the time. But they can collect information about their surroundings and use it to complete specific tasks.

Artificial intelligence is created using computer programs. These programs work together with sensors, **GPS** trackers, and other equipment on a drone. For example, a drone might be equipped with a sensor that recognizes when an object is in front of the drone. Its AI program uses the information from the sensor to adjust the drone's flight path and avoid a collision.

Imagine It!

➡ Make a list of ways AI technology might be able to improve drones.

➡ For example, could AI somehow help prevent drones from crashing? Or help them perform specific jobs?

➡ Think about things that humans aren't very good at. Could a computer do those things better?

Dig Deeper!

✔ Watch a professional drone pilot demonstrate cutting-edge AI drone technology: http://bit.ly/SmartDrones.

✔ Watch a human-controlled drone race against an AI-controlled drone: http://bit.ly/DroneFast.

Artificial intelligence researchers run many test flights with drones.

While today's AI technology is impressive, experts believe that there is still a lot of room for improvement. They want to create more drones that can help human pilots avoid mistakes. They also want to create drones that don't require human pilots at all.

The push to improve AI technology is led by researchers. These forward-thinking scientists conduct a variety of experiments. They might seek out ways to improve existing technology, such as making a drone that is better at avoiding obstacles. They might also test out entirely new concepts.

Researchers aren't always sure their ideas will work, but they always learn something new as they experiment. As they make discoveries, they share their findings with other scientists and engineers. This information can then be used to build new drones and other useful technology.

Future Artificial Intelligence Researcher

Artificial intelligence is a rapidly developing field. Try to stay on top of all the latest advances in AI technology by following the news. If you want to be an AI researcher, you should also start learning about computer programming as soon as you can. It's never too early to start coding, and you'll need to be good at it if you want to help design new AI programs.

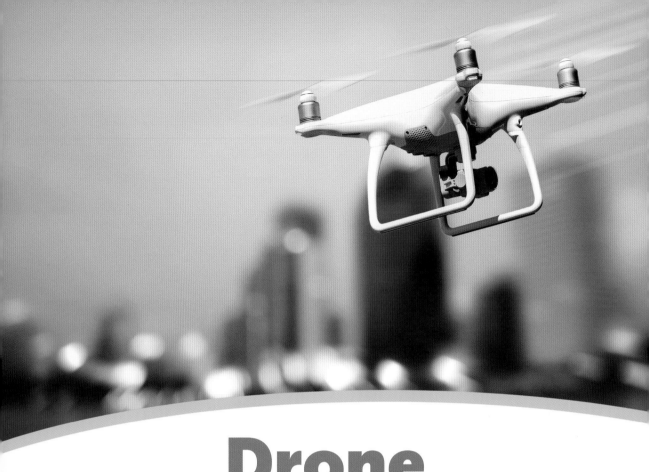

Drone Photographer

Have you ever watched a video where the camera swoops down into a deep canyon or zooms along the side of an icy glacier? How do the filmmakers capture this amazing footage? Today, it's as simple as attaching a video camera to a drone.

One of the greatest advantages of drones is that they can go almost anywhere. They can fly to the tops of mountains or dive off of steep cliffs. Because they are so small, they can also zip through tight spaces that other aircraft cannot. For example, a drone can weave around the trees in a dense forest or zoom through underground tunnels and caves.

Like the latest drones, modern camera technology is also small and lightweight. It can easily be attached to drones. Many drones even come with built-in cameras, allowing users to see from a drone's perspective as they pilot it. This combination of drone and camera technology allows **photographers** and **videographers** to capture images that once would have been impossible.

Some drone photographers and videographers work with filmmakers to create stunning nature **documentaries**. They can use drone-mounted cameras to observe wild animals doing interesting

Imagine It!

- Practice your photography skills.

- Take several pictures of the same subject, but make each one slightly different. Shoot from different angles. Use different lighting. Be creative!

- Make a collage of the photos (either online or on paper). Write a caption for each shot that describes what it is that makes it stand out from the others.

Dig Deeper!

- Watch how a team of videographers use drones to capture rare footage from the inside of an erupting volcano: http://bit.ly/DroneErupt.

Drones can be used to gather weather information.

things, without bothering the animals. They can also capture footage of dangerous natural areas, such as the inside of a volcano. This type of nature footage can be useful to scientists too.

Many businesses hire drone photographers and videographers to help them create ads and marketing materials. For example, drone footage of a beautiful golf course could attract more customers. Aerial photos of a house with a big yard could be included in a real estate listing to help sell the house. Drones are also a great way to capture footage of fast-paced sporting events.

Drone photographers and videographers are more than just pilots. Like any camera operator, they have a good eye for what makes an interesting image. They also have the skills needed to work with the images after they are captured. For photos, this might mean making adjustments using a professional photo editing program. For video, it could involve editing footage together in a way that looks good and makes sense.

Future Drone Photographer

If you want to be good at drone photography, you'll first have to be good at photography in general. Take photos and videos as often as you can, and try to improve your skills all the time. Look online for photography tips, or maybe even take a class. Studying other people's pictures is another great way to learn what makes some photos better than others.

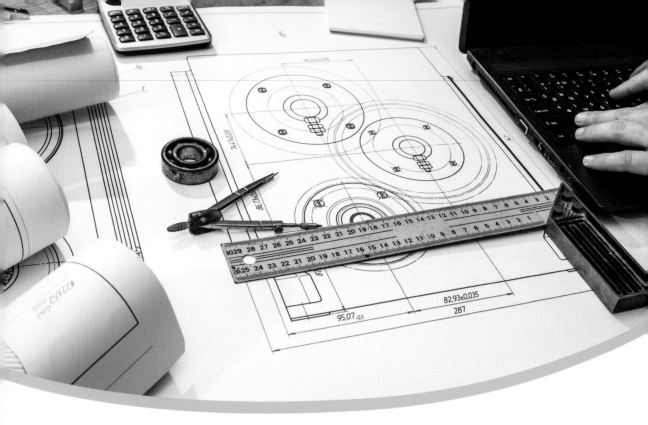

Mechanical Engineer

As you unpack the kit to build your drone, you are amazed at the number of pieces in the box. The drones you've used before didn't seem so complicated. You simply turned them on, and they could fly. But with all these parts laid out in front of you, you can see that it isn't so simple after all!

There is a ton of technology packed into every drone, from the simple ones sold as toys to the state-of-the-art unmanned aerial vehicles UAVs used by the military. Drones have motors, rotors, and other systems needed to make them move. They have sensors to help them take in information about their surroundings. They have batteries to power them and communications equipment that allows them to be controlled from a distance.

Each of the individual parts in a drone was invented by someone. Most were probably the work of creative thinkers called mechanical engineers. Unlike aeronautical engineers, mechanical engineers do not specialize in flight. Rather, these engineers design and build devices of all kinds, from cars to robots.

The **innovations** of mechanical engineers allow aeronautical engineers to create better drones. For example, a team of mechanical engineers might find a way to build a new battery that

Imagine It!

➔ Create your own invention. It could be anything from a new type of vehicle to a useful tool.

➔ Sketch out your ideas on paper.

➔ Now get out some building materials and make a prototype. You can use building toys, art supplies, or anything else you have on hand.

Dig Deeper!

✓ Learn more about the process engineers use to solve problems and design new things: https://www.eie.org/overview/engineering-design-process.

Mechanical engineers figure out how to make drones work.

is smaller and runs longer than existing batteries. Aeronautical engineers could use this development to build lighter drones that can fly faster and farther.

All engineers rely on the same basic process to complete their projects. Everything starts with a problem. For example, maybe engineers think current camera technology is too large and heavy. They would then start brainstorming ways to solve this issue. Can the technology inside the camera be made smaller? Can the camera be built using lighter materials?

Once the engineers have an idea that might work, they start planning and building a **prototype**. This is an early version of an invention that is built for testing purposes. By testing the prototype, engineers can see which aspects of the invention work and which ones need to be improved or fixed. Engineers keep working on their prototypes and building new versions until they finally have a device that solves their original problem.

Future Mechanical Engineer

Though you'll need a college degree to work as a mechanical engineer, you don't have to wait to get started with your own engineering projects. Build things, take things apart, and study how things work. In school, be sure to focus especially hard on math, physics, and other sciences. You'll need this knowledge to be a good engineer!

Software Developer

You've got your new drone unpacked and ready to go. Time for the first flight! You open the drone's app on your smartphone and jump right in. The app is so easy to use that you don't even need instructions. Soon, your drone is zooming through the air and pulling off incredible tricks.

Software is a big part of what makes a drone work. Because pilots are always separated from their drones, they cannot control their aircraft directly. Instead, they rely on a variety of computer programs to communicate with their drones.

If a drone's software doesn't work correctly, then the drone itself doesn't work either. This means a lot of work goes into creating the programs that power a drone. Teams of talented software developers work alongside engineers to create the many programs that are needed. These range from apps to control the drone to artificial intelligence programs that power a drone's **autopilot** features.

Software developers design every aspect of a computer program—from what you see on the screen as you control a drone to the processes that happen inside a drone's "brain." Developers start a project by figuring out which features a program will need. They also decide how users will interact with a program, what the program will look like on-screen, and much more.

Imagine It!

- Imagine you are in charge of creating a smartphone app for controlling a drone.

- Draw rough sketches of what the app would look like on-screen.

- How would the controls work? How would buttons be arranged?

- Try to include as many features as you can without making the app too complicated.

Dig Deeper!

- Play fun games that teach you the basics of coding: https://www.tynker.com/dashboard/student/#/experience/.

- Learn even more with the activities at Code.org: https://code.org/learn.

Software engineers write code that tells drones what to do.

Programming plays a major role in creating software. This is the process developers use to turn their ideas into **code** that a computer can understand. They use special programming languages to create instructions for the computer to follow in different situations. For example, if a user taps a button on a drone app, it might activate a section of code that tells the drone to perform a back flip.

Testing is a very important part of creating good software. Developers try to think of every possible situation that might occur as people use a program. They make sure there are no bugs, or errors, that only happen under certain conditions.

Many programs are never truly finished. Even after they are released to the public, there is always room for improvement. Developers keep working on their programs to fix bugs, add new features, and more. Then they release updated versions of the software.

Future Software Developer

If you want to be a software developer, start by studying the apps and programs you use every day. Learn to think critically about them. What makes certain programs better than others? How could you improve them? In addition, you should learn to code. Programming skills will come in handy no matter what aspect of software development you want to work on.

UAV Pilot

Have you ever seen a movie about a daredevil airplane pilot? It looks like a lot of fun to swoop through the sky, pulling off impressive tricks. But it is also dangerous! With drones, you can get all the excitement of flight while keeping your feet firmly planted on the ground.

Even though pilots of unmanned aerial vehicles (UAVs) don't sit aboard their aircraft, their jobs are not all that different from those of traditional aircraft pilots. They even need many of the same skills and qualities. They need fast reflexes and an understanding of how air movements and different kinds of weather will affect flight.

The type of controls a drone pilot works with can vary a lot depending on the types of drones they use and what their job is. Some drones are controlled using handheld devices that look a lot like video game controllers. Others require pilots to sit in high-tech command centers full of controls and monitors. Even though the pilots are on the ground, their work environment is a lot like the cockpit of an airplane.

Some drone pilots fly solo. They can handle all the tasks involved in piloting their drones without any assistance. Those who fly more complex UAVs, such as state-of-the-art military drones, might work together with several other pilots.

Imagine It!

- ➤ Try flying a drone online!

- ➤ Ask a teacher or parent to help you find and download a "free drone simulator."

- ➤ Practicing online helps you learn without having to worry about crashing a real drone.

Dig Deeper!

- ✔ Watch one of the world's top drone pilots show off his skills: http://bit.ly/DroneBest.

Many people like to fly drones for fun.

Each one is in charge of a specific task. For example, one person might handle the drone's flight path while another controls its weapons systems.

Drone pilots are employed in a wide variety of fields. Perhaps the most well-known is the military. Drones are increasingly crucial in many military operations, from **reconnaissance** to attacks.

You don't have to join the military to become a professional drone pilot, though. Drone pilots work for farmers, police departments, and many other businesses. Some pilots even work in entertainment. They use their drones to put on light shows at concerts, outdoor celebrations, and other events.

If you want to work as a professional drone pilot, you'll probably need to take tests and get a license. Laws vary by location, and new regulations are likely to be put in place as drones become more common.

Future UAV Pilot

The best way to prepare for being a professional drone pilot is to start flying now. You should practice as much as possible with different kinds of drones. As you fly, keep challenging yourself to get better. Set up obstacle courses and try to complete them quickly with no mistakes. Keep track of your times and try to improve them as you repeat a course.

Can You Imagine?

Innovation always starts with an idea. This was true for Alexander Graham Bell, Thomas Edison, Henry Ford, and the Wright brothers. It is still true today as innovators imagine new ways to use drones. And it will still be true in the future when you begin your high-tech career. So ...

What is your big idea?

Think of a cool way to use drones. Write a story or draw a picture to share your idea with others.

Glossary

app (AHP) a computer or smartphone application

artificial intelligence (ahr-tuh-FISH-uhl in-TEL-ih-juhns) the ability of a digital computer or computer-controlled robot to perform tasks commonly associated with humans

autopilot (AW-toh-pye-luht) a device for automatically steering a drone

code (kode) instructions that tell software programs what to do

documentaries (dahk-yuh-MEN-tur-eez) movies or television programs about a real person or events

drones (DROHNZ) unmanned aircraft guided by remote control or onboard computers

GPS (GEE PEE ES) a system of satellites and devices that people use to get directions to a place; GPS is short for global positioning system

innovations (in-uh-VAY-shuhnz) new ideas or inventions

photographers (fuh-TAH-gruh-furz) people who take pictures with cameras for their job

prototype (PROH-tuh-tipe) the first version of an invention that tests an idea to see if it works

reconnaissance (rih-KAHN-ih-sens) a preliminary survey to gain information; especially used by the military to explore enemy territory

software (SAWFT-wair) computer programs that control how computer hardware or technology works

videographers (vid-ee-OG-ruh-furz) people who use cameras to make films

Index

About the Author

Joshua Gregory is the author of more than 125 books for young readers. He currently lives in Chicago, Illinois.